Cavalcade Reflections

Official British Rail Eastern Region Souvenir

Published September 1975 by the Public Relations Dept.,
British Rail, Eastern Region, York

Text and captions set in 10 point Univers Light type,
1 point leaded

Printed by Galava Printing Company Ltd., Nelson

ISBN 0 7003 0029 5

Foreword
by Mr. W.O. Reynolds, O.B.E.,
General Manager, British Rail, Eastern Region

Few among the cheering crowds who saw the opening of the Stockton & Darlington Railway 150 years ago, could imagine the far-reaching influences that railways were to have in the future. Filled with excitement, but also a tinge of awe, they could not realise that this railway, although not the first, was bringing together the elements of passenger railways and establishing what might be described as the prototype for the thousands of railways which were to follow.

Within a few years of this small beginning in North East England, railways spread quickly, first in Britain, and then from Britain throughout the World. The horizons of the masses, confined in the past to journeys by foot or horse, became almost limitless and immense benefits and impetus resulted for the well-being and progress of mankind.

As General Manager of the Eastern Region of British Rail, covering Eastern England from the Thames to the Tweed, and still including in its network most of the Stockton & Darlington Railway, I have a professional interest in this year's 150th Anniversary celebrations. But as a native of the North East, who as a boy, saw the Centenary Cavalcade in 1925 and later began his career with the London & North Eastern Railway,

Foreword continued

this year's event has personal and nostalgic associations, too.

The 1975 Cavalcade, which was staged by the Joint Committee for the Stockton & Darlington Railway 150 Celebrations, on Eastern Region's tracks between Shildon and Heighington, led by the replica of "Locomotion" with British Rail's world's speed record holding High Speed Train bringing up the rear was a kaleidoscope of locomotive progress. It is unlikely that a similar cavalcade will ever be seen again.

I felt that this record of what may well be a unique event should be published and I was pleased to help by lending my support to its production and by contributing this foreword.

I hope "Cavalcade Reflections" will be a valued souvenir faithfully reflecting the 150th Anniversary Cavalcade and one which brings much pleasure to countless readers in the years to come.

Introduction
by William A. Porter

It was Magical Sunday, when Northeast England staged the grandest of all requiems for Steam, when train-lovers of the world pretended, like Kipling might have done, to be "alone wi' God and these, My engines". A Magical Sunday when soccer-sensitive Northeasters banished from their minds dismal Saturday showings by the "Boro" and the "Magpies", both flayed by Lancashire rivals, when "mad dogs" and cricket-loving Englishmen went out in the mid-day sun to forget the predicament of batsmen at the Oval. A Sunday when Britishers could, as only Britishers can, ignore the economic plight of a nation. A Sunday when the Northeast played host to visitors from York and Yokohama, Aberdeen, Amsterdam and Arkansas.

Sunday, 31 August 1975 was the day of the Grand Steam Cavalcade, the glittering climax to celebrations marking the 150th anniversary of the Stockton and Darlington Railway. Here, in the cradle of railwaydom, Northeasters created a once-only day for delving into nostalgia, for sitting in the sun by the lineside, first to chatter in anticipation, then to marvel at the majesty of yesteryear, and finally to reminisce in the twilight long after the Cavalcade had gone. A day for camera-laden devotees to jostle for position on fences along the four-mile Cavalcade route between Shildon and Heighington.

Introduction continued

All roads led to Shildon, gritty railway town where it all began a century and a half ago, and to rural Heighington where George Stephenson's epoch-making "Locomotion" first took to the rails. Shildon had at last written its place into the history of world railways. It had come into its own, first as the centre for a major exhibition, then as the launch-pad for the last great day of steam. Narrow streets thronged with the bearers of railwayana, the collectors of postcards, recordings of locomotive sounds and cans of steam purveyed by those with astute commercial eyes.

Night hours were bliss for steam enthusiasts, oblivious to time as the polishers of locomotives already sparkling like Versailles mirrors. In the pre-dawn at British Rail's engineering works they breathed, with near-sensuous delight, an acrid amalgam of steam and warm oil. It was never like this in the days of steam. The men who sweated for a living in the engine sheds of old would have wondered at the volunteers who tended locomotives as a labour of love. But then, some of the men of steam were there, too, working for fun at the jobs they used to do.

A vast assembly of watchers smiled as a timely sun erased the anxiety of Saturday's teeming rain. The start of the Cavalcade was signalled by a cacophony of sound produced by the whistles of 35 engines blown in unison. Thunderous applause greeted the Cavalcade's leader, a replica of "Locomotion", hauling a chaldron wagon and a Stockton and Darlington passenger coach, footplate crew doffing gleaming toppers to the crowds. Special applause was reserved for renderings of Ilkley Moor Baht 'At by No. 7752 GWR pannier tank engine and GWR's "Raveningham Hall", and ripples of laughter greeted the sight of white-painted coal carried by "Fenchurch". There were engines of every shape and size, from the dwarfish Wantage Tramway No. 5 to the elegant "Flying Scotsman", displaying sponsorship by a brewery. Names that turned back the pages of history steamed by on their slow run to Heighington— "Green Arrow", "Mayflower", "Sir Nigel Gresley", "Henry Oakley", "Hardwicke", "Princess Elizabeth".

At the rear came British Rail's High Speed Train, holder of the world's 143 m.p.h. diesel speed record. As the sleek, streamlined symbol of a new era in rail travel eased, eel-like, out of Heighington with the line clear ahead, one could not but help feel that what had gone down the line before had shown in perspective the results which followed from the first train from Shildon all those years ago.

What will the future hold?

Three o'clock in the morning . . . and the scene at Shildon takes on a surreal atmosphere of misty-eyed dreamland as steam is raised in the shimmering boilers of 30 survivors from another world that is but a memory. They will never gather together again.

The Stockton and Darlington Railway Anniversary has been commemorated on two previous occasions—in 1875 by the Railway Jubilee and in 1925 by the Railway Centenary. Only one locomotive took part in these and in the 1975 Steam Cavalcade, No. 910, a North Eastern Railway 2-4-0 built at Gateshead in 1875, seen here in Shildon Works Yard during the small hours of Sunday, 31 August.

The oddest train running on Cavalcade Day. There were no Press photographers in 1875, and the hand cranked film cameras of 1925 required a firm base from which to operate. Press, Television and Cinema interest in the 1975 Cavalcade was intense. Helicopters, aircraft, hydraulic platforms and two B.R. petrol permanent-way trolleys were pressed into service, securing a unique film record of a unique occasion.

Replica of Stockton and Darlington Railway "Locomotion". In 1925 the original "Locomotion" appeared in the procession propelled by a petrol engine concealed in a replica tender. The mechanical condition of the locomotive 50 years later is such that even this expedient could not be risked. Thanks to the enterprise of Mike Satow and many local engineering firms this working replica was constructed during apprentice training programmes.

Ministry of Supply 0-6-0 Saddle Tank. The desperate shortage of locomotives for use at home and abroad during World War II resulted in the Ministry of Supply commissioning standard designs from private locomotive manufacturers. No. 2502/7 is an example of the shunting type designed and built by the Hunslet Engine Co. of Leeds in 1943. Rugged, simple and making the most economic use of scarce wartime materials, many are still used by N.C.B. and other industrial railways.

London Midland and Scottish Railway 4-6-0 Class 5 MT No. 4767. Named "George Stephenson" by William Whitelaw on 25 August 1975 at a Rail 150 ceremony in Shildon this locomotive is unique. Although the class—known as "Black Fives"—numbered 842 this was the only one with Stephenson valve gear. Built at Crewe in 1947 No. 4767 is now on the North Yorkshire Moors Railway.

North Eastern Railway 0-8-0 Class T2 No. 2238. Built at Darlington in 1918, No. 2238 was one of a class of 120 heavy freight locomotives introduced in 1913. She was one of the last steam engines at work in the North East and has been restored by The North Eastern Locomotive Preservation Group. During restoration, vacuum brakes were fitted for working passenger trains on the North Yorkshire Moors Railway.

North Eastern Railway 0-6-0 Class P3 No. 2392. Class P3 was introduced in 1906 and No. 2392 actually came out of Darlington Works in 1923 during the first year of L.N.E.R. ownership.

Restored by The North Eastern Locomotive Preservation Group, she now works on the North Yorkshire Moors Railway.

London & North Eastern Railway 2-6-0 Class K1 No. 2005. A simplified version of Gresley's three-cylinder K4, the K1 Class was constructed between 1949 and 1950 by The North British Locomotive Company. Although all 70 engines of this type were delivered after nationalisation, the design was pure L.N.E.R. and the present owners, The North Eastern Locomotive Preservation Group have repainted 2005 in apple green as if it had entered service in L.N.E.R. days.

Caledonian Railway 0-4-4 tank Class 439 No. 419. The emblem on the tank side is the Scottish Royal crest which the Caledonian cheerfully adopted as its own without troubling to seek permission. This locomotive, built in Glasgow in 1907, raised a special cheer from Scottish enthusiasts in the grand stands at Shildon. No. 419 can be seen at Falkirk where she is kept by the Scottish Railway Preservation Society.

London & North Eastern Railway 4-4-0 D49/1 Class No. 246, "Morayshire". "Morayshire" was built at Darlington in 1928 and was one of a class eventually comprising 76 engines intended as replacements for elderly locomotives no longer capable of working semi-fast express trains. The last of the class in service, she was withdrawn in 1961 and is now in the care of the Scottish Railway Preservation Society at Falkirk.

Great Western Railway 0-6-0 pannier tank Class 57XX No. 7752, built in 1930 by the North British Locomotive Company in Glasgow. After retirement from British Rail this locomotive worked for London Transport for a time. Its regular home now is the Birmingham Railway Museum, Tyseley. No. 7752 entertained the Cavalcade crowds to a series of tuneful whistle blasts, answered by the other GWR engines.

Great Western Railway 4-6-0 Class 78XX No. 7808 "Cookham Manor". The Great Western Society at Didcot have made a superb job of restoring No. 7808, which although built in 1938, recalls an earlier, more elegant era of locomotive design with her polished brass and copper fittings. The "Manor" Class was the final stage in G.W.R. standardisation policy of using 4-6-0 locomotives for the majority of passenger trains.

Great Western Railway 4-6-0 Modified Hall Class No. 6960 "Raveningham Hall", built at Swindon in 1944. This is one of several locomotives rescued from the "steam engine graveyard" at Barry in Wales by dedicated enthusiasts. It is on view at Steamtown, Carnforth, where restoration was carried out.

London & North Eastern Railway 2-6-2 Class V2 No. 4771 "Green Arrow". Named for the then new L.N.E.R. "Green Arrow" express freight service, No. 4771 was built at Doncaster in 1936. She was the fore-runner of 183 more V2 Class engines which proved so versatile that loco crews called them "the engines that won the war".

"Green Arrow" now has a fitting home in the National Railway Museum at York.

London & North Eastern Railway 4-6-0 B1 Class No. 1306. Not originally named, No. 1306 has been given the name "Mayflower" originally carried by its sister locomotive No. 61379 to commemorate the Pilgrim Fathers. Built in 1948, No. 1306, the last survivor of 410 B1 class engines constructed between 1942 and 1948, is normally on display at Steamtown, Carnforth.

London Midland and Scottish Railway 2-8-0 Class 8F No. 8233. This locomotive had a varied career, beginning with a few months' service for the LMS after construction by the North British Locomotive Company in 1940. Requisitioned by the War Department in 1941 she set sail for the Middle East. Unlike some of her less fortunate colleagues she returned safely to peace-time Britain and served the army at home before joining BR.

War Department 2-10-0 "W.D." Class No. 600 "Gordon" hauling London Transport Departmental electric locomotive No. 12 "Sarah Siddons". "Gordon", like LMS No. 8233, now runs on the Severn Valley Railway, Bridgnorth. No. 600 was built by the North British Locomotive Company in 1943 for the Ministry of Supply. The tender initials stand for Longmoor Military Railway. The electric loco, now a test vehicle for LT, was built for the Metropolitan Railway in 1907 and rebuilt 1922.

London & North Eastern Railway 4-6-2, A4 Class No. 4498 "Sir Nigel Gresley" and Great Northern Railway 4-2-2 Class A1 No. 1. Named after its designer, No. 4498 belongs to the same class as the world steam speed record holder "Mallard". Of an earlier generation of East Coast "Flyers" No. 1, designed by Patrick Stirling, took part in the "Railway Races" of 1888 and 1895, the 1925 centenary procession, and, after a period working special trains in the 1930's, retired to York Railway Museum.

London & North Eastern Railway 4-6-2 A3 Class No. 4472 "Flying Scotsman" and North Eastern Railway 2-4-0 "901" Class No. 910. Probably one of the most famous locomotives in the world, 4472 was built at Doncaster in 1923 and withdrawn in 1963. Since then "Flying Scotsman" has toured America and worked many special trains. Edward Fletcher, designer of No. 910, drove the first train on the Canterbury & Whitstable Railway in 1830. His locomotives were notable for their elaborate and colourful paint schemes.

Great Northern Railway 4-4-2 Class C1 No. 990 "Henry Oakley". Named after the then General Manager of the G.N.R., No. 990 built in 1898 was the first 4-4-2 tender locomotive to run in this country. The engine took part in the 1925 procession, and has only recently been restored to running order after spending 22 years in York Railway Museum.

London and North Western Railway 2-4-0 Precedent Class No. 790 "Hardwicke". The driver and fireman of this Crewe-built locomotive who hurtled her from Crewe to Carlisle in 126 minutes for 141 miles, including Shap, on a "Race to the North" train in August 1895 would have been amazed to think that she would still be able to steam 80 years later. "Hardwicke" is a National Railway Museum engine.

Midland Railway 4-4-0 Compound No. 1000. This locomotive, built at Derby in 1902, gave 49 years active service including front line express work. She headed a group of three maroon engines in the Cavalcade. No. 1000 is one of the magnificent collection in the National Railway Museum, York.

London Midland and Scottish Railway 4-6-0 Jubilee Class No. 5690
"Leander". Built at Crewe in 1937 she was rescued from scrap and rebuilt at
Derby in 1973. Many visitors to the Shildon Rail 150 exhibition commented on
the superb mirror-like finish to this locomotive's paintwork. She can be viewed
at the Dinting Railway Centre, near Manchester.

London Midland and Scottish Railway Princess Royal Class 4-6-2 No. 6201 "Princess Elizabeth". Built at Crewe in 1933 she was to establish a record three years later by scurrying from London to Glasgow in 5 hours 52 minutes, and returning in 5 hours 44 minutes, a time for the 401 miles that was not beaten until after the end of the steam era. The Princess can be seen at Ashchurch.

A venerable group of small locomotives after arrival at Heighington. Wantage Tramway 0-4-0 well tank No. 5, dating from 1857 and believed to be the oldest steamable locomotive in Britain; Lancashire and Yorkshire Railway 0-4-0 saddle tank of 1901, carrying its BR number 51218; and London Brighton and South Coast Railway 0-6-0 tank Class A1X "Fenchurch" built in 1872. No. 5 is now housed at Didcot, No. 51218 is working on the Keighley and Worth Valley Railway and "Fenchurch" is on the Bluebell Railway, Sussex.

Southern Railway 4-6-0 S15 Class No. 841. This locomotive never had a name in its service life, but has now been dubbed "Greene King" after the brewers of a distinctive ale. No. 841 was built at Eastleigh in 1936 and is now to be found on the Stour Valley Railway at Chapel and Wakes Colne.

British Railways 4-6-2 rebuilt Merchant Navy Class No. 35028 "Clan Line".
Although the class was a Southern Railway design this example emerged from
Eastleigh Works after nationalisation in 1948. Originally a distinctive design
with "air-smoothed" boiler casing they were rebuilt by BR, No. 35028 being
given its present form in 1959. Now an attraction at Hereford "Clan Line" used
to be one of Southern Region's top rank locos on expresses to and from
London Waterloo such as "Atlantic Coast Express".

London Midland and Scottish Railway design Class 2MT 2-6-2 tank No. 41241, built by BR at Crewe in 1949. This locomotive's present operators, the Keighley and Worth Valley Railway, have their insignia on the tank sides. Painted a distinctive red 41241 is a great favourite on the preserved line through Bronte country.

London Midland and Scottish Railway design 2-6-0 Class 4 MT No. 43106, built by British Rail in 1951 at former London and North Eastern Railway works in Darlington. Now on the Severn Valley Railway.

British Railways 4-6-0 Class 4 MT No. 75029. Named "Green Knight" since being preserved in 1967, No. 75029 was built in 1954 at Swindon as part of the standard range of locomotives designed by B.R. as replacements for the ageing dozens of different classes inherited from the old companies. "Green Knight" is normally kept at Mr. David Shepherd's East Somerset Railway, Cranmore.

British Railways 2-10-0 Class 9F No. 92220 "Evening Star". Built in 1960, she was the last of 251 heavy freight locomotives constructed during the previous six years and the last steam locomotive built for British Railways. As "Locomotion" and all the other early locomotives were built essentially for hauling coal and iron, it is fitting that the steam age ended where it began—with a rugged, simple machine for moving freight.

The end or a new beginning? As British Rail's record breaking High Speed Train left Heighington, it passed "Locomotion" ready to set off back to Shildon. In terms of railway technology the H.S.T. represents the zenith of the Stephenson system—a self contained power unit, running on steel wheels, on steel rails.

Electrification, body tilting vehicles, slip paved track beds, the abandonment of metal rails, perhaps even the disappearance of the wheel, are all in prospect for railways of the future. We have only reached "The end of the Beginning".

This is the unique front cover of the Special Trains Notice issued to regulate the Cavalcade and Special Trains associated with it.

The following pages carry a facsimile of the Operating Instructions for the exhibits and the petrol permanent way trolleys used as moving platforms for film and television coverage of the event.

BRITISH RAIL
EASTERN REGION

SPECIAL SUPPLEMENT

to

SPECIAL TRAINS NOTICE

in respect of '*RAIL 150*' arrangements

Sunday 31st August 1975

(including overnight train working Saturday/Sunday 30th/31st August and Sunday/Monday 31st August/1st September)

YORK

F. J. BURGE,
Chief Operating Manager,
Eastern Region.

S U N D A Y   3 1   A U G U S T

WORKING INSTRUCTIONS FOR RAIL 150 CAVALCADE
BETWEEN SHILDON AND DARLINGTON (NORTH ROAD)

1. <u>Operating Supervisors</u>

   Operating Supervisors appointed at Shildon, Heighington and Darlington (North Road), are responsible for the regulation and safe working of trains in their respective areas.

2. <u>Suspension of Block Working on Down Line between Heighington and Shildon</u>

   2.1. When the Signalmen at Shildon and Heighington have exchanged "Train out of Section" bell signal for the 13 05 Darlington to Shildon, normal block working on the Down line between Heighington and Shildon will be suspended.

   2.2. After the Operating Supervisors at each place have conferred and satisfied themsleves that the Section is clear, they must instruct the Signalmen to make an entry in the Train Register as follows:-

   > "Block Working over Down line between Heighington and Shildon suspended at   (time)".

   The Signalman and Operating Supervisor at each place must sign the entry.

   2.3. The Signalman at Heighington must then place three detonators 10 yards apart on the Down line at the Signal Box.

3. <u>Arrangements for dealing with Wickham Saloon at Heighington and Suspension of Block Working on the Up line between Shildon and Heighington</u>

   3.1. Special Train 1Z01 formed of the Wickham Saloon will be dealt with in the Up Platform at Heighington. Prior to the arrival of this train, No.37 Points must be placed in the reverse position and secured by clip. When the Operating Supervisor is satisfied that Block Regulation 7A has been applied and that all is in order for the train to proceed to the Up platform it must be handsignalled past No.38 signal.

   3.2. The empty train returning to Darlington must be signalled and dealt with in the normal way.

   When the "Obstruction Removed" bell signal has been exchanged with Shildon normal block working on the Up line between Shildon and Heighington will be suspended.

   3.3. After the Operating Supervisors at each place have conferred and satisfied themselves that the section is clear, they must instruct the Signalmen to make an entry in the Train Register as follows:-

   > "Block Working over Up line between Shildon and Heighington suspended at   (time) for passage of Cavalcade".

   The Signalman and Operating Supervisor at each place must sign the entry.

4.   Suspension of Block Working on Single line between Darlington and Heighington

4.1.   When the Signalmen at Darlington and Heighington have exchanged "Train out of section" bell signal for the empty Wickham Saloon (5Z01) normal block working on the single line between Darlington Signal D840 and Heighington will be suspended.

4.2.   After the Operating Supervisors at each place have conferred and satisfied themselves that the Section is clear they must instruct the Signalmen to make an entry in the Train Register as follows:-

    "Block Working over Single line between Darlington Signal D840 and Heighington suspended at   (time) for passage of Cavalcade in Up direction".

The Signalmen at each place and the Operating Supervisor at Heighington must sign the entries.

4.3.   Points No.1042 at Darlington must be clipped in the reverse position for the passage of the Cavalcade until it becomes necessary to normalise the points for the passage of the H.S.T.

4.4.   During the period of Block Suspension, Rolling Mill and Charity Ground Frames must not be used.

5.   Working of Trolleys Conveying T.V. Cameras and Crews on Down Line between Heighington and Shildon during Suspension of Block Working

5.1.   Two Motor Trolleys conveying T.V. Cameras and crews will enter the section at the Shildon end and will operate within the defined limits shown below, one at the South end and one at the North end of the Section.

5.2.   Before the Trolleys are allowed to enter the section a red banner flag and three detonators 10 yards apart must be placed at the limit of wrong direction movement for the south end Trolley opposite Heighington Down Starting signal (No.35).

5.3.   A Handsignalman must accompany the first trolley to enter the section and upon reaching the 6½ mile post   limiting point the Handsignalman must place two red banner flags 40 yards apart between the North and South Trolley sections and also place three detonators 10 yards apart on the rail between the banner flags. The Handsignalman must then rejoin the trolley.

A Handsignalman must also accompany the second trolley and both Handsignalmen are responsible for ensuring that their trolleys remain within their defined limits during filming and must be prepared to take any necessary protective measures should the need arise.

5.4.   After the passage of the H.S.T. on the Up line or in any case not later than 16 00 hours both Handsignalmen must withdraw the protection on the Heighington side of their respective Trolleys and travel with their Trolleys to the Shildon end of the section. The Handsignalmen must be prepared to take any necessary protective measures during these movements and until the trolleys are removed clear of the running lines at Shildon.

6. Commencement and Progression of Cavalcade

6.1. When the first locomotive of the Cavalcade is departing Shildon the Signalman must send the bell signal 2-2-2 (commencement of Cavalcade), and the Signalman at Heighington must acknowledge and immediately send the signal forward to Darlington who also must acknowledge.

6.2. Movement of Exhibits forming the Cavalcade

6.2.1. The Operating Supervisor at Shildon will regulate the departure of the exhibits in accordance with the details shown in this notice, and will ensure that a minimum time interval of 2 minutes is maintained between successive movements.

6.2.2. Drivers of exhibits should proceed at not more than 5 miles per hour to Heighington, taking care to maintain the appropriate space interval between themselves and the preceding exhibit except at Heighington when:-

(a) those exhibits which are to return to Shildon may be authorised to "close up" on the single line in order to set back onto the Down line.

(b) all exhibits may "close up" towards the colour light starting signal (No.33) when awaiting clearance of preceding exhibits returning to Shildon.

6.2.3. Drivers should sound the whistle/horn before passing each of the T.V. Trolleys which will be operating on the Down line between Shildon and Heighington.

6.2.4. Those exhibits proceding to Darlington may increase speed to not more than 10 mph. on the single line between Heighington and Darlington North Road but must take care not to overhaul the preceding exhibit unless/until they are required to "close up" after entering the Up Goods line at North Road.

6.2.5. Except as provided for above if at any time during the course of the Cavalcade a Driver observes that the preceding exhibit has stopped he must stop also unless/until he is authorised to proceed towards the stationary exhibit. He may however restart without authority if he observes that the preceding exhibit has restarted.

6.3. Change in Formation of Cavalcade

6.3.1. The Operating Supervisor at Shildon must advise forward any variation in the order of the exhibits to that shown in this notice.

6.3.2. The H.S.T. must be the last exhibit in the Cavalcade and should any other exhibit fail to start at the proper time it must under no circumstances be allowed to follow the H.S.T.

6.4. Arrangements at Heighington

6.4.1. After No.37 points have been secured for the movement of the Wickham Saloon (1Z01) from the single line to the Up platform (see para. 3.1.), they must be maintained so secured for the movement of the empty saloon (5Z01) and for the passing of Cavalcade, except as follows.

6.4.2. Upon the arrival at Heighington of an exhibit which is to return to Shildon, a handsignal must be exhibited to stop the exhibit on the single line clear of the points. The handsignalman at Signal No.33 must exhibit a hand danger signal to stop the following exhibit. The Darlington end of the points must then be hand cranked to the normal position and secured by clip for the exhibit to set back to the Down line. The Driver of the first exhibit must be instructed to proceed as far as the marker point near the south end of the down platform and Drivers of subsequent exhibits must be instructed to proceed as far as the line is clear.

6.4.3. When that movement is clear, the Darlington end of the points must then be hand-cranked to the reverse position for the next movement and the handsignalman at No.33 signal may then be authorised to allow the next exhibit to pass that signal at danger and proceed on to the single line.

6.4.4. Should two or more successive exhibits require to return to Shildon, the first must be stopped sufficiently far forward on the single line to allow space for the other/s to stand clear of the points. When all the exhibits returning to Shildon in that group are on the single line the arrangements shown in para. 6.4.2. above must be carried out.

6.4.5. The Operating Supervisor must be in attendance at No.37 Points when these movements are being carried out.

Return of Certain Exhibits from Heighington to Shildon

7.1. At 16 05 hours the exhibits which are waiting at Heighington signal No.36 to return to Shildon on the Down line must be allowed to proceed after removal of the detonators referred to in para 2.3.

7.2. The Driver of the leading locomotive must be reminded by the Signalman that the section may still be occupied by the T.V. Trolleys. The Driver must be prepared to stop short of any obstruction and to run at such speed (maximum 10 m.p.h.) as will ensure that he will not overhaul the T.V. Trolleys preceding him through the section.

7.3. The Driver of the last locomotive, or the rearmost locomotive in the last group, must be given at Heighington a ticket intimating that the locomotive carrying this ticket will be the last exhibit to travel through the section under suspended block arrangements. The movement must be stopped at Shildon signal box to enable the Driver to hand the ticket to the Signalman.

8. Observance of Signals During Suspension of Normal Block Working

  8.1. Shildon

    8.1.1. Main Lines

      Up Main Starting Signal (No.31) will be maintained at Danger
      and Drivers of exhibits may pass it in this position during
      the Cavalcade. All other Main line signals must be obeyed.

    8.1.2. Branch Lines

      Up Branch Home (No.42) and Inner Home (No.40) Signals will
      be cleared for Cavalcade and, except in emergency, will be
      maintained in the clear position for the duration of the
      Cavalcade. All other Branch line signals must also be obeyed.

  8.2. Heighington

    8.2.1. Up Line

      Up Home (No.31) and Up Inner Home (No.32) Signals will be
      cleared for Cavalcade and except in emergency, will be
      maintained in the clear position for the duration of the
      Cavalcade.

      Colour Light Starting Signal (No.35) will be maintained
      at Danger and Handsignalman provided.

    8.2.2. Down Line

      All Down Signals will be maintained at Danger and Drivers
      must act on instructions of Handsignalman or Signalman.

  8.3. Darlington

    8.3.1. Block suspension terminates at Signal D.840. This signal
      or its subsidiary will whenever possible be worked but
      Drivers must be prepared to act on instructions of
      Handsignalman.

    8.3.2. The H.S.T. must only proceed on a main proceed aspect at
      Signal D.840 leading towards Signal D.854.

9. Restoration of Normal Block Working on Up Line Between Shildon and Heighington

  9.1. After the arrival of the H.S.T. at Heighington the Signalman must send "Train
    out of section" signal in accordance with A.B.Reg.6. After this signal is
    acknowledged by the Signalman at Shildon normal working must be restored on the
    Up line.

  9.2. After the Operating Supervisors at each place have conferred and satisfied
    themselves that the section is clear they must instruct the Signalmen to make
    an entry in the Train Register as follows:-

        "Normal Block Working restored over Up line between
        Shildon and Heighington at   (time)"

The Signalman and Operating Supervisor at each place must sign the entry.

10. Restoration of Normal Block Working on Single Line between Darlington and Heighington

10.1. After the arrival of the H.S.T. at Darlington Signal D.854 providing all other track circuits on the Single line are showing clear, the Signalman at Darlington must send "Train out of Section" signal. After this signal is acknowledged by the Signalman at Heighington normal working must be restored on that line.

10.2. After the Operating Supervisors at each place have conferred and satisfied themselves that the section is clear they must instruct the Signalmen to make an entry in the Train Register as follows:-

"Normal Block Working restored over single line between Darlington (North Road) and Heighington at   (time)".

The Signalman at each place and the Operating Supervisor at Heighington must sign the entries.

11. Restoration of Normal Block Working on Down Line Between Heighington and Shildon

11.1. After the Signalman at Shildon has received the ticket carried on the last locomotive over the Down line he must send "Train out of Section" signal in accordance with A.B.Reg.6. After this signal is acknowledged by the Signalman at Heighington normal working must be restored on the Down line

11.2. After the Operating Supervisors at each place have conferred and satisfied themselves that the section is clear they must instruct the Signalmen to make an entry in the Train Register as follows:-

"Normal Block Working restored over Down line between Heighington and Shildon at   (time)".

The Signalman and Operating Supervisor at each place must sign the entry.

12. Whiley Hill Auto Half Barrier Crossing
Between 08 00 and 21 00 this level crossing will be closed to road traffic and ropes and pennants will be erected across the roadway.

"Reflections" by Sydney Martin

Trains of steam—no longer seen
  On lines of iron road;
Heavy monsters breathing fire,
  Manipulating load:
Temperamental—womanlike,
  To men who rode the plate
With hand on regulator,
  To progress! What a fate?
For now they die, their day is done,
  No longer merry song,
Of clanging side-rod—singing wheels,
  Now diesels come along:
They will not die from memory,
  These faithful things of steam
Young men may see their visions—
  But old men still shall dream . . .

Acknowledgements

All photographs published in this book are by Ronald Fletcher, Chief Photographer, British Transport Films, York; Ronald J. Hodsdon, Assistant Chief Photographer, British Transport Films, York; Robert W. Anderson, Photographer, British Transport Films, York and J. Stephen Fountain, Photographer, British Transport Films, York.

  Captions by Allan P. McLean, Regional Press Officer, British Rail, Eastern Region, York and Stuart L. Rankin, Public Relations Department, British Rail, Eastern Region, York.

  Production and Design by Ronald H. Deaton, Public Relations Department, British Rail, Eastern Region, York.

  Issued under the auspices of C. W. F. Cook, Public Relations Officer, British Rail, Eastern Region, York.